Contents

Chapter 1
Families first

A family is one or more adults living together with the child or children they care for. The people in your family have known you since you were born or were very young. They care for you, guide you and share in your life every day. They were there for important events, like when you took your first steps or started at school. They share your joy and your pain, and they care about you more than anybody else in the world does.

FAMILY COUNTS

It does not matter how big your family is. Some families include lots of people, such as grandparents, cousins, aunts and uncles. Some families are smaller. A family can be just two people. Having family to support us through good times and bad can be fantastic. When families get on well, everyone in that family feels happier, safer and more confident.

Having a family around who love you and support you can be a great feeling.

Surviving Your Weird Family

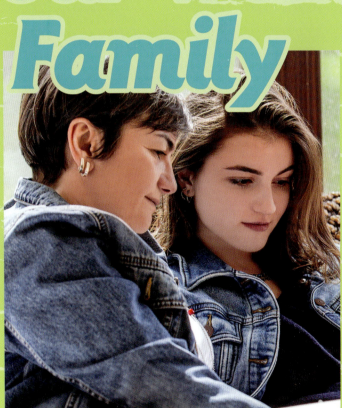

Louise Spilsbury

Raintree is an imprint of Capstone Global Library Limited, a company incorporated in England and Wales having its registered office at 264 Banbury Road, Oxford, OX2 7DY – Registered company number: 6695582

www.raintree.co.uk
myorders@raintree.co.uk

Produced for Raintree by Calcium Creative Ltd
Edited by Sarah Eason, Rachel Blount, and Robyn Hardyman
Designed by Paul Myerscough and Keith Williams
Media research by Rachel Blount
Original illustrations © Capstone Global Library Limited 2021
Production by Spencer Rosio
Originated by Capstone Global Library Ltd
Printed and bound in India
PO1020

978 1 3982 0105 7 (hardback)
978 1 3982 0107 1 (paperback)

British Library Cataloguing in Publication Data
A full catalogue record for this book is available from the British Library.

Acknowledgements
We would like to thank the following for permission to reproduce photographs: Cover: Shutterstock: Pixelheadphoto Digitalskillet; Inside: Shutterstock: Absolute-india 10, Africa Studio 20, AJR Photo 27, Asia Images Group 5, Stephanie Barbary 40, Galina Barskaya 30, Blend Images 44, Digitalskillet 25, DNF Style 7, Dragon Images 11, Iakov Filimonov 42, Glenda 16, Golden Pixels LLC 14, Mat Hayward 19, IgorAleks 28, Patricia Marks 17, MJTH 39, Monkey Business Images 4, 6, 26, 34, 38, 45, Muratart 1, 15, Mark Nazh 24, Nikodash 21, David Pereiras 22, Phoenixns 18, Pixelheadphoto digitalskillet 35, 36, Potstock 13, Pressmaster 31, 37, RyFlip 29, SpeedKingz 9, 43, Threerocksimages 23, Max Topchii 8, Nejc Vesel 33, JP Wallet 12, Tom Wang 41, Lisa F. Young 32

Even families who get on well for the majority of the time may have problems and arguments at times.

FAMILY BLUES

Of course, life is not always perfect, and no family is happy or gets along all the time. When people live together, there are bound to be disagreements. As children get older and want more independence and have different ideas about the world, this may bring them into conflict with their parents. Some family members just have **personality clashes** and always seem to annoy each other. Or sometimes a family that has been getting on well hits trouble when a parent loses their job or gets ill. For most families, there are ways to make things better. Of course, there are some things you can't change. If parents or caregivers have **financial** problems or someone in the family suffers from **alcohol** or **drug** problems, you may not be able to solve those issues yourself. But if everyone in a family does what they can to help the family get on and work through problems – big or small – that family will be stronger.

Different strokes for different folks

There is no such thing as a "perfect" family. Everyone's idea of what makes a family is different. Some families have a mum and a dad, some have parents of the same gender, some have one parent, and when **divorced** parents remarry their new **stepfamily** may be made up of two sets of children. Some families include grandparents, aunts, uncles or friends. Some children live with either mum or dad and go back and forth between their parents' homes. Some children live with a **foster** family. Whatever kind of family you live in, you still have certain **rights** and **responsibilities**.

A family is a loving unit made up of an adult or adults and the children they care for.

WHAT ARE YOUR RIGHTS?

All children have the right to be part of a family that takes care of them. They have the right to somewhere safe to live and sleep, healthy food to eat, clothes to wear and toys to play with. Their family or caregivers should take them to the doctor and dentist when they need to visit, make sure they stay clean and well and get them to school regularly and on time. Children also have the right to live with people who do not hurt or **abuse** them. Most children live with families who love them and give them all the important things they need. If a parent or caregiver cannot provide the proper care or hurts or abuses a child, then the authorities have the right to take action. They can help the parents to do better or find the child a safe place to live.

Some families are made up of adults and the children they have adopted or foster.

WHAT ARE YOUR RESPONSIBILITIES?

As a child in a family, you have the responsibility to respect other family members, obey family rules and to contribute to and cooperate in family life, for example, by doing chores that help the whole family. These can include taking responsibility for your own possessions, tidying your room and sharing some of the chores that keep the house running, like taking out the recycling.

Making it work

Family life can be a bit like riding a rollercoaster. Some weeks it feels great and makes you happy. Other times, family squabbles can drag you down. Families can be tricky, and family life does not always run smoothly, but family is one of the most important things in our life so it makes sense to do what you can to make it work. In this book we look at some of the things you and your family can do to get on better, and to solve problems as they arise.

Spending quality time together is one way families show that they care about each other.

SHOW YOU CARE

There are some things you can start to do right now. For example, some families are always kissing and hugging and saying they love each other. But other people often neglect to say how much they care about each other, maybe because they do not think it needs to be said. It does. Saying and showing you care about each other is really important. Tell your family you love them or – if this feels a bit awkward – tell them how much they mean to you or surprise them with a hug. Other ways in which children and parents can show their love for each other include being polite, thoughtful and respectful of each other every day.

Skills for life

Learning how to **communicate** better with your family day-to-day can improve family relations and can make it easier to sort out problems when they happen. This can be as simple as saying how you feel, honestly and calmly. For example, children often go through times when they would rather be with one parent than the other, or find it easier to talk to one than the other. Explain that although you love them both (if you have two parents), you would like some alone time with one of them.

Sometimes family members argue or misunderstand each other. This can usually be solved by better communication.

Chapter 2
Meet the parents

Your parent or parents, foster-parents, or the other main adult caregivers in your life are hugely important. They are there for you every day and night, and they have a huge impact on how you feel and who you are. Most parents are loving and supportive for most of the time, but there may be occasions when you fall out or you feel like you are always arguing with them.

CLASHING WITH YOUR FOLKS

During **adolescence**, you may find that you get into clashes with your parents about all sorts of things: your friends, the places you go, even the clothes you choose to wear. As you get older and become more independent, some parents react by laying down restrictions. This may make you angry because you feel they don't trust you or don't see things from your point of view. They may also get angry and shout at you in ways you think are unreasonable. It can be tough dealing with parents but don't give up. Try to stick with it and sort out your problems, even if it seems too hard.

Parents can seem frustrating sometimes but they usually act as they do out of love for you.

COMMUNICATION IS THE KEY

Talking to your parents really helps. They may know you very well but they are not mind-readers, so you need to tell them how you feel. Tell them what upsets you and how you would like to be treated. It can help to write about what it is that makes you angry or frustrated. It can be easier to express things in words than to speak directly to someone, especially if you are not getting along well. Writing things down also gives you the chance to read your words back to yourself and make changes before you hand it over to your parents to read.

If your parents are driving you crazy, stop and think about ways you can improve your relationship.

Smothered with love?

Some children struggle with overprotective parents. It's a parent's job to care and worry about us, and to take an interest in our lives and the things we do, but overprotective parents can take this too far. They take over your school project so you can get a better mark or won't let you play outdoors and climb on things in case you fall. These are the parents who worry too much and do too much for us.

WHY YOU NEED SOME SPACE

It is right that parents teach children how to be safe, and some children seem to take stupid risks so they probably need more control. But what if you feel you are sensible and your parents are too protective? Remind them that children need to be allowed to take some risks while they're young so they can grow up to be less fearful and more independent. Children who don't get the freedom to take risks, and explore for themselves may grow up fearful and less confident. By learning to conquer small challenges, we prepare for bigger ones.

Parents can give useful guidance but it's also important to learn how to do some things yourself.

SHOW YOU ARE SENSIBLE

The children who are given more freedom are often the ones who prove they can be trusted with that freedom. They show they are sensible about taking care of themselves and do not take stupid risks. They learn from lessons or instructions, like not to play with knives or run while holding scissors. When parents see that children listen to rules and understand potential dangers, they are more likely to trust them to make sensible decisions and choices for themselves. This extends to your schoolwork too. While it is nice to get support and some help from parents with school projects, it is important that they are your own. That is how you learn. Explain that you need to be responsible for your own work, as it is your subject choices and future that are at stake. They will be impressed by your maturity!

Finding a balance

Getting along with parents is all about finding a balance. Your relationship with them is changing as you grow up, and it helps if you can understand that this is as tricky for them as it is for you. As you get older, they have to change the way they behave with you and let go of the control they have had over you, so it is inevitable there will be conflict sometimes. Remember that although they may seem annoying sometimes, they are doing their best to care for you. They may be finding it hard to let go of the little kid you were, so try to understand where they are coming from. This will help you to see how helping them can help you too.

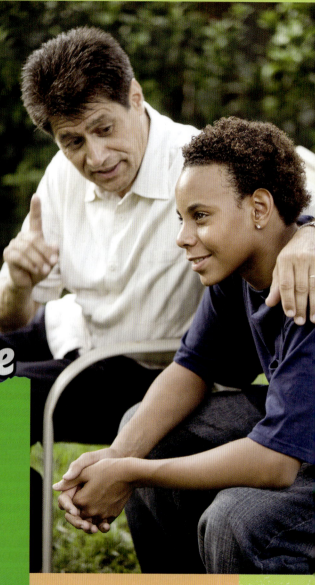

Asking your parents for advice lets them know you respect them and their *opinions*.

Skills for life

If you respect your parents, they will respect you too. You can show respect in different ways. If you ask your parents for help, you show them that you respect their knowledge and experience. You could, for example, ask them to help you choose which classes to take at school or to check over some homework. Notice the things they do for you and thank them. Tell them you are proud of how hard they work or the effort they put into helping everyone in the family.

SHARING TO SHOW CARING

One of the tricky balances you have to find is between getting the privacy you need and letting parents into your life. It is natural that you want some privacy, to share some things only with your friends or to have time alone in your room, to be with your own thoughts or to chat with friends on the phone or online, but you need to make time for your parents too. If you share some information with them and introduce them to your friends, they will feel more a part of your life and understand what is going on with you. By sharing with them, you will show you care for them and they will be more likely to accept that you need your privacy and alone time.

Sharing some information with your parents will make them feel part of your life and more likely to respect your privacy when you ask for it.

Chapter 3
Sibling sorrows

Brothers and sisters, or **siblings**, may get along with each other well most of the time but there are often problems with these relationships too. Siblings know how to annoy each other. They might borrow stuff from each other without asking. Older siblings sometimes feel like the younger children get away with more than they did at that age, and younger siblings might feel annoyed that the older ones get more freedom than they do.

A NEW MEMBER OF THE FAMILY

It's an exciting time when a new baby is born into a family but it can also be tricky to have a new baby brother or sister. Babies need to have everything done for them and they can make a lot of noise when they are hungry or tired. Many children miss having their parents to themselves and miss the way things were before the baby came along. They may feel tired if the baby wakes them up at night. But if you are feeling neglected or not getting enough sleep, tell your parents. They will understand and they should be able to make some changes to make things better for you.

Siblings may get along with each other very well, but most siblings find each other really annoying from time to time!

SIBLING RIVALRY

Try to remember that a newborn baby brother or sister will soon become less demanding and more fun to play with.

Sibling rivalry is competition between siblings. It is the way brothers and sisters compete for a parent's attention or to be the best at something. Sibling rivalry can be a good thing if it makes us work harder at something or strive for better grades in school, but it can also stop siblings from getting along. It is important to be happy for your sibling when they achieve something, like score a goal in a match or win a prize in an art or talent competition. Try not to let feelings of rivalry stop you from saying something nice or congratulating them. We all have different things we are good at. If you can feel happy for them when they succeed, they will feel happy for you when you achieve something too.

Stop the squabbling!

Siblings squabble. It's a fact of life. We all disagree with our friends and family sometimes. That's natural. Siblings might push each other and spoil each other's games or they might borrow each other's stuff without asking. This starts an argument. Sometimes arguments get more heated – and even physical. Siblings might hit, kick or otherwise hurt each other. This is never OK and fighting never solves anything anyway.

If some games trigger arguments, avoid them!

STOP THE FIGHTING

Try to think before you react and take a moment. This should stop you from blowing your top and starting to get physical. Tell your sibling why what they are doing or saying is making you angry, using words. Physical violence only makes things worse; it can hurt one of you and will only get you both into trouble with your parents. Explain clearly to your sibling why they hurt or upset you. If you really feel you cannot control your temper, then walk away.

Skills for life

Count to ten. If you feel anger rising, take a few deep breaths and try doing something like counting to ten.

Ask your sibling to stop the behaviour, in a polite, mature way. Instead of shouting, "Get out of my room right now!" say, "Please come back later, I need some quiet time."

HOW TO STOP A FIGHT

Say what you're feeling and why. So instead of pushing a sibling away, say, "I feel worried that you're going to damage my stuff when you grab it like that."

Walk away. If you feel like you're losing control, leave the room.

Talk about it. If you need help controlling your temper, explain how you feel to trusted adults in your family to see if they can help.

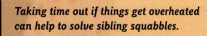

Taking time out if things get overheated can help to solve sibling squabbles.

Time for compromise

It is easy to get caught up in seeing the negatives about a sibling and to forget the bigger picture. Your sibling will be around your whole life, if you are lucky. There will always be squabbles, but if you can find ways to get along better now, then you could be friends forever. Finding a **compromise** means a way of reaching agreement in which each person gives up something that they wanted so they can meet in the middle.

Setting some ground rules with a sibling can make life better for both of you.

GROUND RULES

One way of finding compromises is to set some ground rules between you and your siblings to avoid the squabbling or find ways to stop it when it starts. Ask your siblings to sit down with you and a parent at a time when no one is tired or grumpy. Talk about the things that you often argue about and find compromises to avoid them. For example, you could agree that each of you has a place for your special things and that things in those places must not be touched without permission. Or you could agree to times when you each play a different video game and set a timer when it is time to hand over the controller, or to take turns doing chores at weekends.

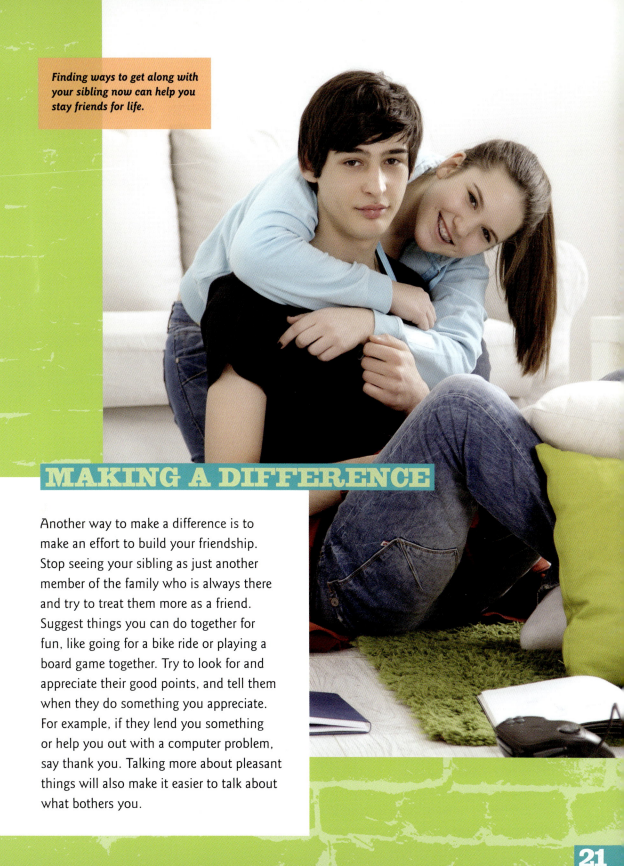

Finding ways to get along with your sibling now can help you stay friends for life.

MAKING A DIFFERENCE

Another way to make a difference is to make an effort to build your friendship. Stop seeing your sibling as just another member of the family who is always there and try to treat them more as a friend. Suggest things you can do together for fun, like going for a bike ride or playing a board game together. Try to look for and appreciate their good points, and tell them when they do something you appreciate. For example, if they lend you something or help you out with a computer problem, say thank you. Talking more about pleasant things will also make it easier to talk about what bothers you.

Chapter 4
Dealing with divorce

When your parents break up, it can be really difficult. Sometimes parents separate or split up after a long period of fighting and unhappiness. Sometimes a **divorce** can seem to happen suddenly, which makes it hard to understand why it is happening at all. When a family breaks up it is usually difficult for everyone. It can make children feel alone, unhappy and unsettled.

It can be very painful when parents decide they do not want to be married to each other any more and want to get a divorce.

WHY DIVORCES HAPPEN

Some parents may have been arguing or unhappy for years before the divorce, so it may be obvious why they have broken up. Some parents do not tell their children what caused a break-up, perhaps because it is too complicated or painful. While this may be understandable, it can be hard for the children, who may end up blaming themselves in some way. Children are never the reason for parents splitting up and they do not cause **separation** or divorce. The reasons that parents get divorced are because they cannot get along or do not love each other any more. If you feel it would help you to understand why the divorce happened, ask your parents to explain as much as they can.

FEELINGS ABOUT DIVORCE

Some children feel angry with the parent who wanted or caused the divorce or feel angry with both parents. This is natural, and it is sometimes made worse by parents who try to get their children to take sides. But try to remember that both your parents love you. Whatever is happening between them does not change the way they feel about you. The pain of a divorce can take a long time to heal, but lots of children go through family break-ups and they do come out the other side able to feel happy again.

Divorce happens in one out of three marriages, so you are not going to be the only child in this situation. Others will understand how you feel.

Coping with change

Change happens in everybody's life but a family break-up brings big changes that can be really hard to get used to. One of the biggest changes is how much and how often you see your parents. Chances are that in the future you will see your parents separately, and since one parent usually moves into a new place, it is also likely that one of them won't live with you any more. You might share your time between two homes or you might live with one parent and visit the other parent. You might see each parent for about the same amount of time or you might see one more than the other. When you have lived with both parents as a family your whole life, this can be pretty tough but it will get easier.

A family break-up can make you feel like your world has ended but things can, and do, get better.

THINGS THAT STAY THE SAME

In the first months after a family break-up, it helps if you can try to be flexible and accept that you will have more hassle to deal with for a while. Many of the changes that happen will take some time to get used to but most if not all of them will feel better with time.

It can help to remember that some of the most important things about your family stay the same after a break-up. Your parents are still your parents and they still love you just the same. That does not change. They might live somewhere new and you might see them less but they are the same people they have always been.

Skills for life

Help yourself by talking about the changes that upset you. Tell your parents how you feel. They may not be able to change things back again but talking it through should help. If your parents make a decision that you are not happy with, talk to them about it. If you have trouble talking to your parents, talk to a **counsellor** or another trusted adult.

Communicating with your family will help you work through any feelings you have.

Focus on the positive

A life-changing event like a divorce can put people through some tough times but these painful feelings will lessen with time. Some children find that tough experiences like divorce can also help them learn about their own strengths and help them to deal with other difficult situations in the future. They learn how to be caring and **empathetic** people who are able to help others as well as themselves.

Over time, some divorced parents begin to get on well and may still get together for family events.

DIVORCE CAN MAKE LIFE BETTER

Some children come to realize that divorce was the best decision for the family and they respect how brave it was of their parents to make that decision. If parents are unhappy together this can affect the whole family, so when parents separate the whole family is happier. In families where parents were fighting a lot before they split up, children may be relieved that the fighting is over. Some children find that they even get to spend more time with one or both of their parents than they did before, and so get to know them better. If parents are happier when they are not together, they might be more fun to be with.

LIVING YOUR LIFE

Of course, even if there are some things that are better after a divorce, the break-up of a family is still very painful. To cope with the hurt and stress, it's important to live your life to the fullest and make sure you get on with the things you enjoy. Sports and exercise help you to relax and to let your feelings out, so get out there and get moving. Read books, watch films or play with your pet. Do not feel guilty about having fun at this sad time; it's important. Spend time with friends too. Some children find it hard to tell their friends about their parents splitting up but good friends can help you feel better, and it will help them to understand why you are sad or distant sometimes.

It takes time, but trust that one day things will start to feel more "normal" again.

Chapter 5
Sorting out stepfamilies

After a divorce, your parents might start dating other people. After a while, they may even marry again or start living with their new partner. The new partner may have children of their own from a previous relationship as well. You might become part of a stepfamily, with new stepsiblings.

A NEW FAMILY

Getting used to being part of a different kind of family, or two new families if both your parents remarry, can be difficult. Some children still hold on to the hope that their parents may get together again, so when they remarry this dream is shattered. Some children feel rejected when a parent is interested in a new partner and their children, and feel left out or abandoned. They can feel sad or even angry that they have to share their parent with the new partner and their children. Children may not like the new partner or their children, and feel like they never want to be in the new, shared, stepfamily home.

When divorced parents remarry, children can find they belong to two new families.

WHEN STEPFAMILIES WORK

Getting used to being part of a stepfamily takes time and effort, and if everyone tries hard to make things work there are lots of positives about being part of a stepfamily. For example, after spending time with just one parent or the other, some children enjoy feeling like they are part of a big family again. They often feel pleased to see their mother or father happy again, with a new partner. Having another adult around can make them feel safer too. In a stepfamily there are more adults and perhaps other children to talk to or to do things with, especially if there are more grandparents and other relatives to care about them.

Building new relationships

Making good friends takes time and effort, and in a new stepfamily it will take time for everyone to get used to each other. It's important for both the children and the adults to try to make things work while they get used to living together, and learning different ways of doing things.

NEW STEPPARENTS

Children can feel like their new stepparent is too strict or wants to change everything, or even does not care about them. Maybe the stepparent is trying too hard while they try to make the new family work. They may want to make new rules for the new family, and that can be tough too. Some stepparents may try to be too affectionate or friendly too soon. If that is the case, then try to explain calmly that you need time to get used to this new family set-up. It will take you some time to get used to a parent who does things differently, but you will get there.

Making an effort to talk to and get along with a new stepparent can make all the difference.

NEW STEPSIBLINGS

It is pretty normal for there to be tension between new stepsiblings. You might be very different kinds of people, and used to doing things differently at home. Suddenly you have to share your lives and sometimes even a bedroom. You may feel jealous of your parent's relationship with their new stepchildren too. Try to be reassured that they love you just the same, and they are just trying to help everyone get along. Try to get to know your new sibling and take an interest in their interests. When you have a problem, talk it over with them calmly and **constructively** instead of bottling up your feelings. Of course, it is still OK to ask a parent for some time alone with them when you need it.

One way to build a good relationship with a stepsibling is to find a hobby or activity that you can both enjoy together.

Dealing with your feelings

While getting used to being part of a new stepfamily, most children experience a whole range of different feelings and emotions. They might feel jealous and want their parent all to themselves. They might worry that if they like a new stepparent, this will make their own parent feel replaced or left out. They might feel angry that a stepparent treats them unfairly, and gives them more chores or criticism than their own children.

If you think you're being given more chores than a stepsibling, talk to your parents about it.

SOLVING PROBLEMS

Every family has problems from time to time. To solve these problems, everyone needs to listen to each other and be prepared to compromise and think about the other person's point of view. Think carefully about how you feel. Could you be mistaking being treated differently for being treated unfairly? Are you being asked to do more chores simply because you are older, for example? You may have to be prepared to put up with some changes and try not to get overly upset about smaller changes. Think about the things that really matter to you, and express yourself honestly to your parents so they can help you work out how to deal with it.

Writing down the way you feel can be a great release and makes feelings of sadness, anger and pain less intense.

Skills for Life

- **Have family meetings.** Getting together every week to discuss plans and problems and sharing thoughts or opinions openly can help stepfamilies work better.
- **Let it out.** If you feel angry towards a stepparent, try writing down your feelings in a journal rather than taking it out directly on them.
- **Talk about it.** Speak about your feelings to friends, relatives or anyone you trust.
- **Be specific.** Think about exactly what real problems there are and talk to your parents about how to sort them out. Make a list if you need to. You may decide that some seem less important when you write them down.
- **Get help.** If things are really bad, you might want to see a family counsellor to help your family work out how to get on.

Chapter 6
Let's talk about it!

Communication is the key to making any relationship work, and talking to your parents, siblings and other relatives about the things that matter is one sure-fire route to happier families.

Families who play together stay together!

GETTING TOGETHER

It's easy for family members to get caught up in their own activities and worries and treat each other as housemates, passing on the stairs. They may find they talk to each other only about the things they have to, such as practical details about getting to activities or whose turn it is to feed the pets. That is why regular family meals are important. They are a chance to talk and share quality time together. Make sure you get involved in family traditions too, like a weekly game or a family pizza night, even when everyone seems too busy for everything else.

COMMIT TO CONVERSATIONS

When you have time together, make an effort to engage in conversation with your family. You can ask each other basic questions, such as how their day or week is going. During dinner, everyone can share one piece of both good news and bad news from the day or take turns sharing a joke. Daily chats like this are a great time to talk about the little things that happen in our lives. They are also a chance for you to ask your parents questions – for example about their work or what they would like to do at the weekend. It doesn't matter too much what you end up talking about. The point is to spend time showing that you are as interested in learning about them as they are in you and that you care about them as people.

Conversations with families matter, even if you're not talking about anything very important.

Speak and listen

To communicate effectively with your family there are several things you can do. For one thing, try not to start a conversation in an angry way, by shouting or yelling at your parents or by whining about something. If you do this, it makes people think that you are less mature than you are and it tends to make them less likely to take what you say seriously.

THINK BEFORE YOU SPEAK

When you have something to say, it is easy to blurt the words out without thinking about what you really mean or want to say. It can make a big difference to take a few moments to think about what you want to say and how it will sound to the person you are speaking to. For example, if a parent does or says something that upsets you, tell them about it and how it makes you feel but try to say it calmly and kindly. Your parents make mistakes too, and like all of us may do or say things they did not mean. If you speak to them in the right way they are more likely to think carefully about what you have said. Thinking before you speak reduces the risk of misunderstandings.

Listening respectfully is mature behaviour and will make people more likely to listen thoughtfully to you.

HOW TO BE A GOOD LISTENER

It is also important to learn to be a good listener. One way to do this is to look people directly in the eyes when they are talking and not interrupt them. If you are not sure what they mean, ask them to repeat it or repeat back what you understood them to mean. For example, you could say, "So you mean, if I get all my homework done I can go and play football for an hour before dinner?" Being a good listener also means putting away your mobile phone or closing your laptop while you are having a conversation with someone. It can be really difficult to listen properly to someone if you are doing something else, and it makes them feel ignored too.

If you don't look at people when they talk it suggests you're not listening or don't care what they are saying.

Coping with conflict

While some conflicts are inevitable, the way they play out depends a lot on how we deal with them. One of the most important things you can do to stop an argument escalating out of control is to avoid making it too personal. Try to avoid statements like "You're such a grumpy parent" or "You never listen to me anyway". The person you are talking to will feel like you're just attacking them. Try to start statements with the word "I". For example, "I feel upset and left out of things at school the next day when I'm not allowed to see my friends". Saying how you feel when something happens makes the whole exchange less personal and challenging.

Try to talk about troubles rather than shutting family members out.

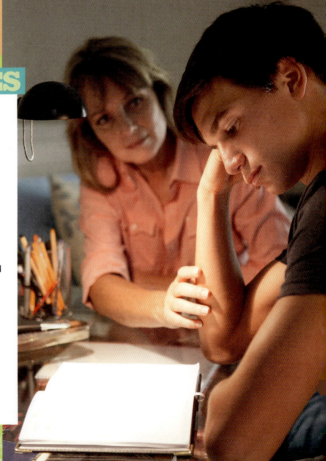

TRADING PLACES

It can also help to put yourself in the other person's position and try to look at the conflict from their perspective. Try to imagine how you would feel if you were in their situation. For example, have they just got in from work and therefore likely to be more tired and unreasonable at the moment? Or can you see how they might be worried for your safety if you do a certain thing? Trading places is not about changing your mind. It's about understanding why you disagree and caring about the other person's point of view. This will help you figure out how to talk about the conflict too, because you can address their points.

Getting out for a run or some other form of exercise when times are tough can help to clear your head and help you to see things more clearly.

Skills for life

If conflicts start to get nasty, take a break and agree to continue the discussion later. Suggest that everyone needs some time to calm down and some space to think about the argument from both sides. In the time out, consider doing something relaxing to help you calm down, like going for a walk or having a shower.

Your voice counts

As you get older, you will have more opinions and ideas of your own. You may want to discuss these with your family or you may feel that you do not want to talk about them in case your parents or family do not agree with you. You have the right to express your opinion without being put down, just as they have the right to express theirs. It's OK to disagree with people and to have different opinions.

If your parents have opinions that you do not agree with, understand that this is OK, and try to remain respectful.

THE RIGHT TO AN OPINION

Most parents are happy to believe that they teach their children to think for themselves. They want you to be a thoughtful, caring person who considers decisions and choices carefully, weighing up the **pros** and **cons** of different situations you encounter and figuring out what to do based on your own ideas and **morals**. But sometimes parents are still shocked when this means we develop ideas and opinions different from theirs! In fact, every child has the right to express their views and have them taken seriously. The **United Nations** made sure this right was included in their **Convention on the Rights of the Child**. Children should be included in discussions about issues that affect them, at home and in the world.

AGREE TO DISAGREE

If you are in a discussion with parents or other members of the family about something, try to resist making it into an argument about who is right and who is wrong. If, for example, the conflict is about an aspect of **society**'s values or beliefs, it is possible that you will never agree. For example, if you have a different idea from your parents about what a politician is doing, that's OK. In many families, mums and dads vote differently in elections from each other. It is good to discuss these issues but there is no need to get into a fight about it. You could suggest agreeing to disagree. This means that they agree to let you have your opinions and you agree they have the right to keep theirs.

You have the right to form your own opinions and the right to be heard.

Family meetings

Family meetings are meetings in which family members gather together to make family decisions or discuss problems. Families can use these meetings to resolve particular arguments or problems that have happened or to discuss things like house rules and holiday plans. If you think family meetings are a good idea, talk to your parents and make sure you choose a time for them that works for everyone. Also, choose somewhere to hold the meeting where everyone can be comfortable and sit together, such as around the dinner table. Make sure distractions like the TV and mobile phones are switched off so you can all concentrate on talking and listening to each other.

Family meetings allow everyone in a family to share their opinions, find solutions to problems and understand each other better.

GROUND RULES

At your first meeting, it is good to establish a set of ground rules. You can come up with these together, and they should be rules that everyone understands and agrees to follow. These rules could include things like:

- Everyone gets a turn to have their say, even if others do not agree with what they say.
- One person talks at a time and does not get interrupted.
- It is OK, and important, to say what you feel.
- No one has to talk but everyone has to listen when someone is talking.
- No one puts anyone else down and there should be no shouting or name-calling.

SOME THINGS YOU COULD DISCUSS

People discuss a whole range of things at family meetings. They take time to recognize the good things happening in the family, distribute chores fairly for the week ahead or make plans for a family outing. These can also be times for talking about issues like sibling rivalry. In discussions of problems, both sides should give their view and everyone can suggest ways to solve the problem. Talk about the pros and cons of each solution and together come to an agreement about the best one.

Some families have agendas for family meetings. An agenda is a list of things to talk about.

Family matters

Families come in all shapes and sizes and can be made up of people who are related to you by blood or not, but one thing all families share is their importance. Family matters because your family is made up of people who accept you for who you are and who love you no matter what. Your family will stay with you in difficult times and be there to support you with their love and care. A family makes all its members feel safe, gives them a big part of their identity and helps to build their values.

Every member of a family has an important part to play in making that family work.

BEING PART OF A FAMILY

Being part of a family means pitching in and trying to make life better for each other. If your family argues sometimes, try not to worry. Arguments happen and they are a part of learning how to live with each other and get along. Even the happiest homes have problems sometimes. Do your best to make your family work and encourage and take part in talking about and solving any family problems. Working out how to make family relationships thrive will help you later in life if and when you have a family of your own.

Skills for life

If you are being physically, **sexually** or emotionally abused or neglected by anyone in your family, you must take action to make it stop. That is the only way you can be safe and well. If there is someone else in your family you trust, talk to them and ask them to help you get the support you need. There are also groups of people outside the family who can help you sort out problems of abuse in your family. Organizations such as Childline can be contacted by a phone hotline, and you will be able to talk to a counsellor in confidence.

If there are problems in your family that you cannot handle or you are being hurt or threatened in any way by a family member, there are people and organizations you can turn to for help. You have the right to be cared for properly so get help if you need it.

Glossary

abuse to treat someone with cruelty or violence, especially regularly or repeatedly

adolescence the time in a child's life when they go through puberty and become an adult

alcohol a powerful substance in drinks such as wine or beer that can affect your body, lifestyle and mental health

biological connected by blood rather than by adoption or marriage. A mother and father who produced you are your biological parents.

communicate to share information with others in some way. We communicate by speaking, writing, moving our hands and body or using other signals.

compromise an agreement between two sides who have different desires or opinions, in which each side gives up something it had wanted. For example, if two people want to watch different films, they might compromise and choose another that they both like.

cons the disadvantages or the case against an argument

constructively done in a way that will help to develop or improve something

Convention on the Rights of the Child an international law that states that children up to the age of 18 years should be given special protection and assistance by the countries they live in and the people who care for them

counsellor a person who is trained to give advice and help people with their problems

divorced the status of a person when his or her marriage has legally and officially ended

drug a substance that causes a change in the body. When a person takes drugs that are not medicines it may make them angry, ill or sad, for example.

empathetic able to understand and share another person's feelings

financial to do with money

foster bring up a child that is not one's own by birth

ground rules basic rules that everyone agrees to follow

morals accepted ideas of right and wrong

opinions views, judgements or beliefs that someone holds about a particular matter

personality clashes situations in which two or more people do not get along very well because they have very different characters or personalities

pros advantages or aspects in favour of something in an argument

responsibilities things you should do

rights things that people are legally (by law) or morally (by a sense of what is right and just) entitled to

separation when two people who are still married live separately, sometimes during the period leading up to a divorce

sexually when someone touches the area usually covered by your underwear. Sexual abuse is when this happens inappropriately (for example, between an adult and a child) or in a way that makes a child feel uncomfortable or scared.

siblings brothers and sisters

society people who live together in an organized community with shared laws, traditions and values

stepfamily a family that is formed on the remarriage of a divorced or widowed person, and that includes a child or children

United Nations an international organization formed in 1945 to increase political and economic cooperation among its member countries

Further Reading

BOOKS

Relationships (Teen Issues), Cath Senker (Raintree, 2013)

Siblings: You're Stuck with Each Other, So Stick Together, James J. Crist and Elizabeth Verdick (Free Spirit Publishing, 2010)

The Hidden Story of Family Break-Ups (Undercover Story), Sarah Levete (Raintree, 2017)

WEBSITES

Childline
childline.org.uk
Childline's counsellors offer support for children under 19 years old either online or on the phone 24 hours a day, 7 days a week.

Family Action
www.family-action.org.uk/
Family Action provides practical help and support to families who may be struggling through poverty or social isolation

Sibling Support
www.siblingsupport.co.uk/
This charity gives support and advice to children on the death of a sibling

Young Minds
youngminds.org.uk
Young Minds is a leading mental health charity.

Note to parents and teachers: the Publishers have made every effort to recommend websites that are from trustworthy sources and that are age-appropriate for the readers of this book. However, due to the changing nature of the internet, we cannot be responsible for content shown on these pages and we recommend that all websites are viewed under the supervision of a responsible adult.

Index